SECURE YOUR FUTURE

A Comprehensive Retirement Savings Guide

Suze Kaufman

Pegmans Publishers

Copyright © 2024 Suze Kaufman

All rights reserved

The ideas portrayed in this book are for information and wakeup call purposes only. It is adviced you do your own research or seek expert opinion of retirement options available for you.

No part of this book may be reproduced, or stored in a retrieval system, or transmitted in any form or by any means, electronic, mechanical, photocopying, recording, or otherwise, without express written permission of the publisher.

Cover design by: McStephens Graphics
Printed in the United States of America

To all those who dream of a future filled with financial security and peace of mind: May this guide serve as a beacon of knowledge and empowerment as you navigate the path to a fulfilling retirement. Your dedication to securing your future is an inspiration to us all.

CONTENTS

Title Page
Copyright
Dedication
Book Description
Introduction
PART 1: UNDERSTANDING RETIREMENT SAVINGS
Chapter 1
Chapter 2
PART 2: RETIREMENT SAVINGS OPTIONS
Chapter 3
Chapter 4
Chapter 5
Part 3: Investment Strategies for Retirement Savings
Chapter 6
Chapter 7
Chapter 8
Part 4: Maximizing Your Retirement Savings
Chapter 9
Chapter 10
Chapter 11
Part 5: Putting It All Together
Chapter 12
Chapter 13
Chapter 14
Conclusion
Glossary of Retirement Savings Terms

References
Afterword
About The Author

BOOK DESCRIPTION

Are you ready to take control of your financial destiny and secure a fulfilling retirement? Look no further than "Secure Your Future: A Comprehensive Retirement Savings Guide." In today's uncertain economic landscape, planning for retirement has never been more crucial. This essential guide provides a road-map to navigate the complexities of retirement planning with confidence and foresight.

From estimating expenses and income to understanding the intricacies of employer-sponsored retirement plans and individual retirement accounts (IRAs), this book covers it all. Learn how to leverage tax-advantaged accounts, manage risks, and build a diverse portfolio that ensures long-term financial security.

Whether you're just starting your career or nearing retirement age, "Secure Your Future" offers actionable insights and practical advice to help you craft a personalized retirement savings plan. Dive into topics like asset allocation, diversification, and ongoing portfolio monitoring to optimize your retirement journey.

But remember, "Secure Your Future" is not an expert insight or investment guide. It's a wake-up call to start planning for your future retirement. Readers are encouraged to do their own research and seek expert opinions to develop strategies that suit their individual needs.

Don't wait until it's too late. Start planning for your future today with "Secure Your Future: A Comprehensive Retirement Savings Guide."

INTRODUCTION

Retirement savings stand as a pivotal pillar of financial planning, with their significance now greater than ever. With the incessant surge in living costs, prolonged life expectancy, and the precariousness surrounding social security, seizing control of one's financial destiny becomes imperative (Kijakazi, 2022). Crafted adeptly, a retirement savings blueprint not only assures tranquility but also furnishes financial stability, affording individuals the liberty to pursue their passions during their golden years (Fidelity Investments, 2022).

Citing a recent study by the National Institute on Retirement Security (NIRS, 2022), the median retirement account balance for individuals aged 55–64 barely scrapes $120,000, a sum inadequate for fostering a comfortable retirement. This stark revelation underscores the exigency for an exhaustive guide, one that offers pragmatic counsel and expert discernments on retirement savings.

Purpose and scope:

This book embarks on a mission to furnish a comprehensive and easily digestible roadmap to retirement savings, emboldening readers to take command of their financial destinies. Our objective is to enlighten and apprise individuals on the multifaceted realm of retirement savings, delving into investment strategies, tax advantages, and risk mitigation methodologies.

Throughout the course of this thesis, we will delve into the following pivotal themes:

Grasping the gamut of retirement savings avenues, encompassing employer-sponsored schemes and individual retirement accounts (IRAs).

Illuminating investment blueprints tailored for retirement savings, embracing asset allocation methodologies, and diversifying strategies.

Harnessing tax perks while assiduously trimming down on fees and penalties.

Crafting a resilient and sustainable retirement income stream.

This compendium is tailored to cater to individuals across all age brackets and income strata, from neophytes embarking on their professional journeys to those teetering on the brink of retirement. Our endeavor is to furnish a lucid and succinct manual that shepherds readers through the labyrinthine landscape of retirement savings, equipping them with the requisite tools to realize their financial aspirations.

PART 1: UNDERSTANDING RETIREMENT SAVINGS

CHAPTER 1

Why Retirement Savings Matters
The Retirement Savings Crisis

Retirement savings stand as a pivotal cornerstone of financial planning, yet the grim reality persists: many individuals falter in setting aside ample resources for their twilight years, thereby engendering a retirement savings crisis (Kijakazi, 2022). This crisis manifests in a glaring deficit in retirement funds, leaving a substantial cohort of workers ill-prepared for their golden years (NIRS, 2022).

The Consequences Of Not Saving Enough

The repercussions of inadequate retirement savings are dire, encompassing: Financial Insecurity: An insufficiency in retirement savings precipitates financial insecurity, coercing retirees into leaning heavily on meager

Social Security benefits or resorting to government aid (SSA, 2022).

Diminished Standard of Living: Without a robust retirement nest egg, retirees may find themselves grappling with a marked downturn in their standard of living, compromising their overall quality of life (Fidelity Investments, 2022).

Heightened Family Burden: Paltry retirement savings elevate the burden on family members, who may find themselves compelled to extend financial support to their aging loved ones (AARP, 2022).

Limited Healthcare Options: Inadequate retirement savings curtail access to quality healthcare services, imperiling the physical and mental well-being of retirees (Kaiser Family Foundation, 2022).

Elevated Stress and Anxiety: Financial insecurity during retirement fosters heightened levels of stress and anxiety, exacting a toll on retirees' mental health (American Psychological Association, 2022).

The Importance Of Retirement Savings

Retirement savings assume paramount importance for several compelling reasons: Financial Autonomy: It bestows upon retirees the gift of financial autonomy, liberating them to pursue their interests and passions without the specter of financial constraints (Kijakazi, 2022).

Comfortable Retirement: A judiciously amassed retirement fund promises a retirement characterized by comfort, enabling retirees to uphold their accustomed standard of living (Fidelity Investments, 2022).

Healthcare and Long-Term Care: Adequate retirement savings serve as a bulwark against healthcare and long-term care expenses, ensuring retirees access to top-tier medical services (Kaiser Family Foundation, 2022).

Legacy Building: Retirement savings pave the path for legacy building, affording retirees the peace of mind that comes with securing the financial future of their progeny (AARP, 2022).

In summation, retirement savings emerge as the linchpin for a secure and gratifying retirement. The ramifications of failing to amass sufficient savings are manifold, spanning from financial vulnerability to compromised well-being. Thus, it behooves individuals to accord primacy to retirement savings and seize control of their financial destinies.

CHAPTER 2

Understanding Your Retirement Needs

Estimating Expenses And Income In Retirement

Embarking on effective retirement planning necessitates a meticulous comprehension of one's future expenses and income streams. This entails prognosticating living costs, healthcare expenditures, and miscellaneous outlays while also pinpointing potential sources of revenue (Kijakazi, 2022).

Expenses In Retirement

Housing: This encompasses rent or mortgage payments, property taxes, and insurance premiums (NerdWallet, 2022).

Food and Transportation: It spans groceries, dining out, and transportation expenses (BLS, 2022).

Healthcare: This category comprises medical bills, insurance premiums, and potential long-term care costs (Kaiser Family Foundation, 2022).

Entertainment and Travel: Encompassing hobbies, travel ventures, and leisure pursuits (AARP, 2022).

Debt Repayment: This involves settling outstanding debts, such as credit card balances and loans (Federal Reserve, 2022).

Income In Retirement

Social Security Benefits: monthly stipends disbursed by the Social Security Administration (SSA, 2022).

Retirement Accounts: Withdrawals from 401(k), IRA, or pension schemes (Fidelity Investments, 2022).

Pensions and Annuities: Assured income emanating from employer-sponsored plans or annuity contracts (Kijakazi, 2022).

Part-time Work: Income derived from part-time employment or consultancy endeavors (Gallup, 2022).

Factors Affecting Retirement Savings

Numerous variables can exert influence on one's retirement savings, including:

Inflation: The escalating cost of living can diminish purchasing power over time (BLS, 2022).

Investment Returns: Fluctuations in the market can impact the growth trajectory of retirement accounts (Fidelity Investments, 2022).

Healthcare Costs: Escalating medical expenses pose a threat to retirement savings (Kaiser Family Foundation, 2022).

Longevity: Increased life expectancy augments retirement expenses (SSA, 2022).

Debt: Outstanding debts can impede retirement income (Federal Reserve, 2022).

To ensconce oneself in a comfortable retirement, it is imperative to:

Accurately Estimate Expenses and Income

Cognizance of Factors Impacting Retirement Savings

Formulate a holistic retirement plan.

By gauging one's retirement needs astutely, individuals can blueprint a bespoke strategy to safeguard their financial futures.

PART 2: RETIREMENT SAVINGS OPTIONS

CHAPTER 3

Employer-sponsored plans (401(k), 403(b), etc.)
How They Work, Benefits, And Limitations

Employer-Sponsored Plans Overview

Employer-sponsored retirement plans, such as the ubiquitous 401(k) and 403(b) arrangements, stand as linchpins of retirement savings for countless individuals (Investopedia, n.d.). These plans offer a seamless and tax-efficient avenue for amassing funds earmarked for retirement, encapsulating an array of benefits and constraints that warrant a nuanced understanding.

How Employer-Sponsored Plans Work

Employer-sponsored retirement plans represent vehicles through which employers extend retirement savings opportunities to their workforce (Kijakazi, 2022).

Contributions, typically deducted from employees' paychecks, may be complemented by employer-matched contributions (Fidelity Investments, 2022). These contributions find their way into diverse investment vehicles, spanning mutual funds, stocks, and bonds, fostering growth that is sheltered from immediate taxation (Forbes, 2022).

Benefits Of Employer-Sponsored Plans

Tax Advantages: Contributions to these plans enjoy tax deferral, effectively paring down taxable income (Kijakazi, 2022).

Employer Matching: Some employers offer matching contributions, effectively augmenting employees' savings with additional funds (Fidelity Investments, 2022).

Compound Interest: Contributions accrue interest over time, harnessing the power of compounding to bolster account balances (Forbes, 2022).

Retirement Savings: These plans furnish employees with a structured vehicle for fortifying their retirement reserves, fostering financial security in later years (Kijakazi, 2022).

Limitations Of Employer-Sponsored Plans

Contribution Limits: The IRS imposes caps on annual contributions to these plans, constraining the extent of potential savings (IRS, 2022).

Vesting Requirements: Certain plans necessitate employees to fulfill tenure-related criteria before gaining full ownership of employer contributions (Investopedia, n.d.).

Withdrawal Penalties: Premature withdrawals prior to age 59 1/2 may incur penalties and tax liabilities (IRS, 2022).

Investment Risks: Investments within these plans carry inherent risks, rendering account balances susceptible to market fluctuations (Forbes, 2022).

Recent Research And Findings

Recent research conducted by the Employee Benefit Research Institute underscores the positive correlation between participation in employer-sponsored plans and heightened retirement savings rates (EBRI, 2022). Furthermore, insights gleaned from a study by Fidelity Investments reveal that sustained contributions to these plans over a decade or more culminate in median balances exceeding $200,000 (Fidelity Investments, 2022).

In summation, employer-sponsored retirement plans emerge as indispensable tools in the arsenal of retirement planning, furnishing employees with a conduit to fortify their financial futures. A comprehensive comprehension of these plans, encompassing their mechanics, benefits, and limitations, empowers employees to navigate their retirement savings journey with sagacity and prudence. By leveraging the perks of employer-sponsored plans and judiciously navigating their constraints, individuals can chart a course toward financial serenity in retirement.

CHAPTER 4

Individual Retirement Accounts (IRAs)
Traditional And Roth IRAs: Contribution Limits And Rules

Overview of Individual Retirement Accounts (IRAs)

Individual Retirement Accounts (IRAs) emerge as a favored avenue for retirement savings, endowing individuals with tax advantages and maneuverability (Investopedia, n.d.). Delineated into traditional and Roth variants, each IRA harbors distinctive contribution limits and regulatory parameters.

Traditional IRAs

Traditional IRAs give individuals the latitude to funnel pre-tax dollars into their retirement coffers, effectively paring down their taxable income (Kijakazi, 2022). Contributions nestle and burgeon tax-deferred until withdrawal, at which juncture they are taxed as ordinary income (IRS, 2022).

Contribution Limits:

$6,000 in 2022, or $7,000 if 50 or older (IRS, 2022).

Rules:

Contributions are tax-deductible.

Withdrawals are taxed as ordinary income.

Required Minimum Distributions (RMDs) are obligatory after 72 years of age (IRS, 2022).

Roth IRAs

Roth IRAs afford individuals the opportunity to channel post-tax funds into their retirement corpus, with contributions germinating and proliferating sans tax encumbrance (Forbes, 2022). Withdrawals bear no tax implications under specific conditions.

Contribution Limits:

$6,000 in 2022, or $7,000 if 50 or older (IRS, 2022).

Rules:

Contributions originate from after-tax dollars; they are not tax-deductible.

Withdrawals are tax-exempt if:

Account maturity spans at least 5 years.

Withdrawal occurs after 59 1/2 years of age.

Withdrawal is designated for a maiden home acquisition or qualified educational outlay (IRS, 2022).

Recent Research And Findings

Recent analyses conducted by the Investment Company Institute underscore that IRAs collectively boasted $11.6 trillion in assets by 2021's denouement, with 43% of households harboring IRA holdings (ICI, 2022). Additionally, insights gleaned from a study by Fidelity Investments reveal that individuals who steadfastly contribute to IRAs over a decade or more accrue median balances surpassing $100,000 (Fidelity Investments, 2022).

IRAs emerge as veritable linchpins in the tapestry of retirement planning, offering individuals a pliable and tax-efficient conduit to fortify their financial futures. A cogent comprehension of the contribution limits and stipulations governing traditional and Roth IRAs empowers individuals to navigate their retirement savings trajectory with acumen and foresight. By availing themselves of IRAs and leveraging their attendant tax perks, individuals can forge a path toward financial solvency in retirement.

CHAPTER 5

Annuities and Other Retirement Income Sources
Fixed And Variable Annuities; Other Options (E.g., Pensions, Social Security)

As individuals edge closer to retirement, the quest for dependable income sources to complement retirement savings becomes paramount (Kijakazi, 2022). Annuities and alternative retirement income avenues offer a steady stream of income, assuaging apprehensions regarding asset depletion in later years (Forbes, 2022).

Annuities

Annuities, or contractual arrangements with insurance entities, offer a guaranteed income stream spanning a specified duration or lifelong tenure (Investopedia, n.d.). Two primary types of annuities delineate this landscape: fixed and variable.

Fixed Annuities: Fixed annuities furnish a secured interest rate and a steadfast income flow, thereby affording predictability and principal safeguarding (Kiplinger, 2022).

Variable Annuities: Variable annuities pivot on diversified asset investments, wherein income flux is contingent upon investment performance (Forbes, 2022). While harboring growth potential, they concurrently entail exposure to investment vicissitudes.

Other Retirement Income Sources

Pensions: Pensions and employer-sponsored initiatives furnish a guaranteed income reservoir hinged on years of service and terminal salary benchmarks (PBS, 2022).

Social Security: Social Security, administered by governmental agencies, dispenses a predetermined income stream predicated on lifelong earnings (SSA, 2022).

Recent Research And Findings

Recent scrutiny by the Society of Actuaries underscores the efficacy of annuities in assuaging retirement income vagaries (SOA, 2022). Moreover, insights gleaned from research by the Employee Benefit Research Institute posit that individuals endowed with pensions and Social Security benefits exhibit augmented retirement income security (EBRI, 2022).

Annuities and alternative retirement income sources furnish a bedrock of stability, thereby fortifying individuals against financial precariousness in retirement. A nuanced understanding of diverse annuity categories and ancillary options empowers individuals to craft judicious retirement income frameworks. By fostering income source diversification, individuals can forge resilient retirement income architectures conducive to enduring financial well-being.

PART 3: INVESTMENT STRATEGIES FOR RETIREMENT SAVINGS

CHAPTER 6

Asset Allocation and Diversification
Building A Balanced Foundation For Your Future

In the previous chapters, we've explored the importance of setting retirement goals, understanding your time horizon, and the power of compound interest. Now, it's time to translate that knowledge into action by building your retirement portfolio. This chapter dives deep into the concepts of asset allocation and diversification, the cornerstones of a secure financial future.

Why Retirement Savings Matter

According to a 2022 report by the Employee Benefit Research Institute (EBRI), a staggering 26% of American workers have nothing saved for retirement (Employee Benefit Research Institute, 2022). This statistic highlights the critical need for proactive planning. Social Security benefits alone are often insufficient to maintain your desired lifestyle after retirement (Social Security Administration, 2023). Building a robust retirement nest egg allows you to live comfortably and pursue your passions in your golden years.

Purpose And Scope Of This Chapter

The purpose of this chapter is to provide guidance on how to effectively save and invest for retirement in order to achieve financial security and peace of mind. It specifically focuses on the art of asset allocation and diversification, two strategies crucial for building a balanced and resilient portfolio.

Understanding Risk And Return

Investment decisions are a constant balancing act between risk and return. Risk refers to the possibility of losing money on your investments. Conversely, return signifies the potential gain on your invested capital. Generally, higher potential returns are accompanied by greater risk. Understanding your risk tolerance—your comfort level with potential losses—is paramount when building your portfolio.

A 2023 study published in the Journal of Pension Economics & Finance found that a significant portion of retirement planning errors stem from individuals misjudging their risk tolerance (Fernandes & Lusardi, 2023). This chapter will guide you through assessing your risk tolerance and aligning your investment strategy accordingly.

Creating A Balanced Portfolio: The Power Of Asset Allocation

Asset allocation refers to the strategy of dividing your investment portfolio across different asset classes. These asset classes typically include:

Stocks represent ownership in companies and offer the potential for high long-term returns, but they also carry higher risk.

Bonds: Issued by governments and corporations, bonds offer a steady stream of income (interest payments) and are generally considered less risky than stocks.

Cash Equivalents: Highly liquid assets like money market accounts and short-term certificates of deposit (CDs) offer minimal risk and low returns.

By strategically allocating your investments across these asset classes, you can create a balanced portfolio that aligns with your risk tolerance and time horizon. A younger investor with a longer time horizon can typically tolerate a higher allocation toward stocks for their growth potential, while someone nearing retirement might prioritize stability with a greater allocation towards bonds and cash equivalents.

Diversification: Spreading Your Eggs Across Multiple Baskets

Diversification is the practice of investing in a variety of assets within each asset class. This principle minimizes the impact of any single investment's performance on your overall portfolio. For example, within the stock asset class, you can diversify by investing in companies across different sectors like technology, healthcare, and consumer staples.

A 2021 research paper published in The Quarterly Review of Economics and Finance emphasizes the importance of diversification in mitigating portfolio risk (Bawa, 2021). The paper highlights that diversification helps to reduce the volatility of your portfolio, protecting you from significant losses if any particular investment performs poorly.

In summation, asset allocation and diversification are fundamental building blocks for a secure retirement. By understanding your risk tolerance and allocating your investments across different asset classes, you can create a balanced portfolio that weathers market fluctuations and positions you for a comfortable retirement. The following chapters will delve deeper into specific investment options and strategies to help you construct your ideal portfolio.

CHAPTER 7

Investment Options for Retirement Savings

Building Your Nest Egg With Confidence.

Congratulations! You've grasped the importance of retirement savings and mastered the concepts of asset allocation and diversification. Now, it's time to explore the exciting world of investment vehicles that will make your retirement dreams a reality. This chapter dives deep into various investment options suitable for retirement savings, empowering you to make informed decisions and build a robust portfolio.

Why Retirement Savings Matter

As discussed earlier, Social Security benefits alone are unlikely to sustain your desired lifestyle after retirement (Social Security Administration, 2023). According to a

2023 report by the Pew Research Center, nearly half of all retired Americans (45%) rely on Social Security as their major source of income (Pew Research Center, 2023). Building a nest egg through smart investments allows you to supplement Social Security and maintain financial independence in your golden years.

Purpose And Scope Of This Chapter

We've covered the foundational aspects, like setting goals and managing risk. Now, this chapter focuses on the practical tools you'll need to construct your portfolio—a variety of investment options.

Investment Options: A Spectrum Of Choices

The investment landscape offers a diverse range of options, each with its own risk-return profile. Here's a breakdown of some popular investment choices suitable for retirement savings:

Stocks represent ownership in companies and offer the potential for high long-term capital appreciation. However, they also carry the risk of stock price fluctuations.

Bonds: Issued by governments and corporations, bonds provide a steady stream of income (interest payments) with lower risk compared to stocks.

Diversification Through Investment Vehicles

While individual stocks and bonds can be directly purchased, most investors utilize investment vehicles that offer diversification and convenience.

Exchange-Traded Funds (ETFs): These are passively managed baskets of securities that track a specific index or market sector. ETFs offer low fees, diversification, and easy tradability on stock exchanges (Investopedia, 2023).

Mutual funds are professionally managed pools of money that invest in a variety of assets, like stocks, bonds, and commodities. Mutual funds offer diversification and expertise but may come with higher fees compared to ETFs.

Index funds are a specific type of mutual fund that passively tracks a particular market index, aiming to mirror its performance. Index funds typically have lower fees than actively managed mutual funds (The Balance, 2023).

Choosing The Right Investment Option

The ideal investment mix for you depends on your individual circumstances, risk tolerance, and time horizon. Younger investors with a longer time horizon can generally handle a higher allocation towards growth-oriented assets like stocks (through ETFs or index funds) to maximize their potential returns. As you near retirement, your portfolio might shift towards more conservative options like bonds to prioritize income and stability.

Additional Considerations: Beyond Stocks And Bonds

While stocks and bonds remain the cornerstone of most retirement portfolios, you may also consider diversifying into other asset classes depending on your risk tolerance and investment goals. Here are a few examples:

Real Estate Investment Trusts (REITs): Invest in income-producing real estate properties, offering potential for rental income and long-term capital appreciation.

Commodities: Include assets like gold, oil, or agricultural products in your portfolio for further diversification, but be aware of their higher volatility.

This chapter has explored various investment options suitable for retirement savings. Remember, the key is to choose a mix of investments that aligns with your risk tolerance and time horizon. The following chapters will delve deeper into investment strategies and provide guidance on constructing a well-diversified retirement portfolio.

CHAPTER 8

Managing Risk and Protecting Your Savings

Safeguarding Your Future

The path to a secure retirement isn't without its challenges. Even the most meticulously crafted investment plan can encounter bumps along the way. This chapter equips you with the knowledge to navigate potential risks and safeguard your hard-earned savings. We'll explore common retirement planning risks, along with strategies to mitigate their impact and protect your financial future.

Why Retirement Savings Matter

Remember, relying solely on Social Security is unlikely to sustain your desired lifestyle after retirement (Social Security Administration, 2023). A 2022 study by the National Institute on Retirement Security (NIRS) found that retired couples need an average of $1 million saved to maintain a comfortable retirement (National Institute on Retirement Security, 2022). Building a robust retirement nest egg allows you to weather financial storms and maintain your desired standard of living in your golden years.

Purpose And Scope Of This Chapter

Throughout this journey, we've covered essential topics like setting goals, understanding risk tolerance, and building a diversified portfolio. This chapter focuses on the ever-present reality of risk and equips you with strategies to manage it effectively.

Understanding And Mitigating Retirement Planning Risks

Several key risks can threaten your retirement savings:

Inflation: Over time, inflation erodes the purchasing power of your money. A dollar today won't buy the same things as it will in the future. Inflation risk can be mitigated by strategically allocating your portfolio towards assets that historically perform well in inflationary environments, such as certain stocks and real estate investment trusts (REITs) (The Motley Fool, 2023).

Market Volatility: Stock markets experience periods of both growth and decline. While short-term fluctuations shouldn't derail your long-term strategy, excessive fear during market downturns can lead to impulsive decisions that harm your portfolio. Maintaining a diversified portfolio and staying invested for the long term are crucial for weathering market volatility (Schwab, 2023).

Longevity Risk: Living longer than anticipated can deplete your retirement savings. A 2023 report by the Society of Actuaries projects a continued rise in life expectancy in developed countries (Society of Actuaries, 2023). Carefully considering your life expectancy when planning your retirement income needs is essential.

Hedging And Insurance Strategies: Building Your Safety Net

While risk cannot be entirely eliminated, proactive strategies can help you manage its impact.

Hedging is using investment strategies to offset potential losses in other parts of your portfolio. For example, using options contracts can hedge against stock market downturns. However, hedging strategies can be complex and require a solid understanding of the financial markets.

Insurance: Certain insurance products can protect your retirement savings from unforeseen events. For example, long-term care insurance can help cover the costs of assisted living in case of future health needs. Disability insurance can replace lost income if you become unable to work due to illness or injury.

Risk management is an integral part of any successful retirement plan. By understanding potential risks and implementing strategies like diversification, asset allocation, and appropriate insurance, you can build a resilient portfolio that safeguards your financial future. The following chapters will delve deeper into specific retirement planning strategies and considerations to help you achieve your retirement goals with confidence.

PART 4: MAXIMIZING YOUR RETIREMENT SAVINGS

CHAPTER 9

Unleashing the Tax Advantage
Maximizing Your Retirement Savings

Retirement planning isn't just about saving money; it's about saving it strategically. The good news is that the government offers a variety of tax-advantaged retirement accounts that can significantly boost your nest egg. This chapter dives deep into these accounts and explores strategies to maximize their benefits, allowing you to keep more of your hard-earned money for your golden years.

Why Retirement Savings Matter

As discussed earlier, Social Security alone likely won't maintain your desired lifestyle after retirement (Social Security Administration, 2023). A 2021 report by the Center for Retirement Research at Boston College found that retirees with employer-sponsored retirement plans have a significantly higher median retirement income compared to those who rely solely on Social Security (Center for Retirement Research at Boston College, 2021). Maximizing your retirement savings through tax-advantaged accounts allows you to accumulate a larger nest egg and enjoy a more comfortable retirement.

Purpose And Scope Of This Chapter

We've explored essential topics like setting goals, understanding risk tolerance, and building a diversified portfolio. This chapter focuses on the power of tax-advantaged accounts and strategies to maximize their benefits for a more prosperous retirement.

Tax-Deferred Growth And Withdrawals: Saving Now, Paying Less Later

Many retirement accounts offer tax-deferred growth. This means contributions you make are typically tax-deductible, lowering your taxable income in the year you contribute. The money then grows within the account on a tax-deferred basis. Taxes are only applied when you withdraw funds in retirement (Internal Revenue Service, 2023). This allows your money to compound faster and grow significantly over time.

Popular Tax-Advantaged Accounts

Traditional IRAs: Offer tax-deductible contributions for most individuals with income limitations. Withdrawals in retirement are taxed as ordinary income (Internal Revenue Service, 2023).

401(k)s are employer-sponsored retirement plans that allow salary deferrals (pre-tax contributions) and often come with employer-matched contributions. Similar to traditional IRAs, withdrawals in retirement are taxed as ordinary income (Internal Revenue Service, 2023).

Roth Accounts: Paying Taxes Now for Tax-Free Growth

Roth accounts offer a different tax advantage: tax-free, qualified withdrawals in retirement. Contributions to Roth accounts are typically not tax-deductible, but any qualified withdrawals made after age 59½ and upon holding the account for at least five years are tax-free and penalty-free (Internal Revenue Service, 2023).

Roth Conversions and Other Strategies: Optimizing Your Tax Benefits

Depending on your income tax bracket and retirement goals, Roth conversions can be a powerful strategy. A Roth conversion involves converting funds from a traditional IRA or 401(k) to a Roth account. While you'll pay taxes on the converted amount in the year of conversion, you'll enjoy tax-free qualified withdrawals in retirement. Consulting with a financial advisor can help you determine if a Roth conversion is a suitable strategy for your situation (The Motley Fool, 2023).

Tax-advantaged retirement accounts offer a significant advantage when planning for your future. By leveraging tax-deferred growth and considering Roth accounts and conversions, you can significantly increase your retirement savings and keep more money in your pocket. The following chapters will delve deeper into retirement income strategies and considerations to help you translate your savings into a secure and fulfilling retirement.

CHAPTER 10

Supercharge Your Savings
Catch-Up Contributions And Savings Boosters

The path to retirement security isn't always linear. Life throws curve-balls, and sometimes starting to save for retirement feels like climbing a mountain. But fear not! This chapter equips you with powerful strategies to accelerate your retirement savings, particularly if you're starting later or want to give your nest egg an extra boost. We'll delve into catch-up contributions and explore creative ways to increase your retirement savings and reach your financial goals.

Why Retirement Savings Matter

Remember, relying solely on Social Security is unlikely to maintain your desired lifestyle after retirement (Social Security Administration, 2023). A 2023 report by the

Employee Benefit Research Institute (EBRI) highlights a concerning trend: nearly half of all working Americans (47%) report having no retirement savings or less than what they feel they need (Employee Benefit Research Institute, 2023). Regardless of where you are on your savings journey, it's never too late to take action. This chapter empowers you with strategies to catch up and build a secure retirement.

Purpose And Scope Of This Chapter

This chapter focuses on strategies to accelerate your retirement savings, particularly for those who may be starting later or want to maximize their contributions.

The Power Of Catch-Up Contributions: A Retirement Savings Advantage

The good news is that the IRS recognizes that some individuals might need to save more aggressively later in their careers. For those aged 50 and above, many retirement plans offer "catch-up contributions." These allow you to contribute additional amounts above the standard contribution limits, accelerating your retirement savings significantly (Internal Revenue Service, 2023).

Traditional IRA Catch-Up: Individuals aged 50 and over can contribute an additional $1,000 per year to their traditional IRA in 2023, with the limit increasing to $3,000 in 2024 for those aged 55 and over (Internal Revenue Service, 2023).

401(k) Catch-Up: Many employers offer 401(k) plans with catch-up contributions. In 2023, the catch-up contribution limit for individuals aged 50 and over is $7,500 (Internal Revenue Service, 2023).

Beyond Catch-Up Contributions: Additional Savings Strategies

Catch-up contributions are a powerful tool, but they're not the only way to boost your retirement savings. Here are some additional strategies to consider:

Increase Your Regular Contributions: Even small increases to your regular contributions can significantly impact your retirement savings over time due to the power of compounding interest. Consider automating your contributions to make saving a seamless part of your budget.

Revisit Your Budget: Analyze your spending habits and identify areas where you can cut back. Reallocating those funds towards your retirement savings can make a big difference.

Consider Side Hustles: Explore ways to generate additional income through freelance work, a part-time job, or a side hustle. Dedicate this extra income towards your retirement savings for an accelerated boost.

Max Out Employer Matching: If your employer offers a retirement plan with a matching contribution, prioritize contributing at least enough to receive the full match. This is essentially free money that can significantly bolster your retirement savings.

Building a secure retirement requires a proactive approach. Don't be discouraged if you're starting later or want to save more aggressively. By leveraging catch-up contributions, exploring additional savings strategies, and maximizing employer benefits, you can significantly accelerate your retirement savings and achieve your financial goals. The following chapters will delve into the world of retirement income planning, helping you translate your accumulated savings into a secure and fulfilling retirement.

CHAPTER 11

Keep more of what you earn.
Avoiding Fees And Penalties In Retirement Savings

Building a secure retirement requires careful planning and smart investing. However, hidden fees and potential tax penalties can eat away at your hard-earned savings over time. This chapter empowers you to become a savvy investor by helping you understand common retirement account fees and penalties, along with strategies to minimize their impact. By keeping more of your money working for you, you can significantly boost your retirement nest egg.

Why Retirement Savings Matter

As discussed earlier, Social Security alone likely won't sustain your desired lifestyle after retirement (Social Security Administration, 2023). A 2022 study by the

Transamerica Center for Retirement Studies found that the average retiree needs $1.7 million saved to live comfortably in retirement (Transamerica Center for Retirement Studies, 2022). Every dollar saved and invested strategically makes a significant difference in achieving your retirement goals. Minimizing fees and penalties allows you to maximize your retirement savings and reach financial independence sooner.

Purpose And Scope Of This Chapter

This chapter focuses on the often-overlooked aspect of fees and penalties associated with retirement accounts. By becoming a more informed investor, you can make smarter choices and keep more of your money on track for a secure retirement.

Demystifying Retirement Account Fees: Different Fees For Different Needs

Retirement accounts come with various fees that can significantly impact your returns over time. Here are some common fees to be aware of:

Expense Ratios: Mutual funds and ETFs often have annual expense ratios that cover the costs of managing the fund. Lower expense ratios translate to higher returns for you (The Balance, 2023).

Account Fees: Certain retirement accounts may charge annual maintenance fees or transaction fees. Shop around for accounts with low or no fees.

Investment Management Fees: If you utilize a professional financial advisor to manage your retirement portfolio, they may charge management fees based on a percentage of your assets.

Understanding Penalties And Avoiding Early Withdrawals

Early withdrawals (before age 59½) from most retirement accounts typically incur a 10% penalty in addition to income taxes (Internal Revenue Service, 2023). This can significantly erode your savings. There are some exceptions to this penalty for qualified expenses like medical bills or a first-time home purchase, but it's crucial to understand the rules to avoid costly mistakes.

Strategies To Minimize Fees And Penalties

Choose Low-Cost Index Funds: Index funds typically have lower expense ratios compared to actively managed mutual funds (Investopedia, 2023).

Compare Fees Before Investing: Don't settle for the first retirement account you come across. Research different options and compare expense ratios, account fees, and investment minimums.

Consider Robo-Advisors: Robo-advisors are automated investment platforms that offer low-cost investment management services, particularly suitable for those comfortable with a do-it-yourself approach.

Work with a Fee-Only Advisor: Financial advisors who charge fixed fees or hourly rates may be a good option to receive personalized investment guidance without hidden fees.

Plan for Long-Term Growth: A long-term investment horizon allows you to ride out market fluctuations and avoid the temptation of withdrawing funds early and incurring penalties.

Fees and penalties can be a silent drain on your retirement savings. By understanding the different fees associated with retirement accounts, becoming a more informed investor, and implementing strategies to minimize their impact, you can keep more of your money working for you. The following chapters will delve into the world of retirement income planning, helping you translate your accumulated savings into a secure and fulfilling retirement.

PART 5: PUTTING IT ALL TOGETHER

CHAPTER 12

Charting Your Course
Creating A Personalized Retirement Savings Plan That Aligns With Your Goals And Financial Situation.

The path to a secure retirement starts with a roadmap. This chapter empowers you to create a personalized retirement savings plan tailored to your unique financial goals and circumstances. We'll guide you through the essential steps of setting clear goals, determining your time horizon, and strategically allocating your assets to build a well-diversified investment portfolio.

Why Retirement Savings Matter

Social Security alone is unlikely to maintain your desired lifestyle after retirement (Social Security Administration, 2023). A 2023 report by the Pew Research Center highlights a concerning trend: nearly two-thirds of

Americans (63%) express anxiety about not having enough money for retirement (Pew Research Center, 2023). Building a robust retirement nest egg through a well-defined savings plan allows you to face retirement with confidence and financial independence.

Purpose And Scope Of This Chapter

This chapter focuses on the crucial step of crafting a personalized retirement savings plan—your roadmap to financial security in your golden years.

Building Your Personalized Plan: A Step-By-Step Guide

Creating a personalized retirement savings plan requires careful consideration of several factors:

Step 1: Defining Your Retirement Goals: What kind of lifestyle do you envision in retirement? How much income will you need to cover your expenses comfortably? Clearly define your retirement goals to determine the amount you need to save (The Balance, 2023).

Step 2: Assessing Your Time Horizon: When do you plan to retire? Knowing your time horizon helps determine your investment strategy. Younger investors with a longer time horizon can generally handle a more aggressive asset allocation, while those nearing retirement may prioritize income and stability.

Step 3: Calculating Your Current Savings: Take stock of your current retirement savings across various accounts (401(k), IRA, etc.). Knowing your starting point is crucial to determining how much additional saving is necessary.

Asset Allocation: Building A Diversified Portfolio

Once you've defined your goals and time horizon, it's time to build your investment portfolio. Asset allocation, the process of dividing your investments among different asset classes, plays a critical role in managing risk and maximizing returns. Here's a breakdown of some common asset classes:

Stocks offer the potential for high long-term capital appreciation but also carry a higher risk of volatility.

Bonds provide a steady stream of income (interest payments) with lower risk compared to stocks.

Cash Equivalents: Include money market accounts and short-term bonds, offering easy access to funds and low risk.

General Asset Allocation Guidelines

Younger investors typically have a longer time horizon and can handle a higher allocation towards growth-oriented assets like stocks (through ETFs or index funds) to maximize potential returns (Investopedia, 2023).

Investors Nearing Retirement: may shift their portfolio towards more conservative options like bonds to prioritize income and stability while still maintaining some growth potential.

Remember: Asset allocation is a personalized strategy. Your risk tolerance, time horizon, and individual circumstances should all be considered when constructing your portfolio. Consulting with a financial advisor can be beneficial to determine the optimal asset allocation for your unique situation.

Creating a personalized retirement savings plan is the cornerstone of achieving financial security in your golden years. By setting clear goals, understanding your time horizon, and strategically allocating your assets, you can build a robust portfolio that empowers you to face retirement with confidence. The following chapters will delve deeper into retirement income strategies and considerations to help you translate your savings plan into a reality, ensuring a comfortable and fulfilling retirement.

CHAPTER 13

Keeping Your Course
Monitoring And Adjusting Your Retirement Savings Plan

The path to a secure retirement isn't a straight line. Life throws curveballs, and your financial situation can evolve over time. This chapter emphasizes the importance of regularly reviewing and adjusting your retirement savings plan to ensure it remains aligned with your evolving goals and circumstances. By proactively monitoring your progress and making strategic adjustments, you can keep your retirement dreams on track.

Why Retirement Savings Matter

Remember, relying solely on Social Security is unlikely to sustain your desired lifestyle after retirement (Social Security Administration, 2023). A 2022 study by the Retirement Income Institute found that retirees underestimate their healthcare costs in retirement by an average of $12,000 per year (Retirement Income Institute, 2022). Building a robust retirement nest egg allows you to weather unexpected expenses and maintain your desired standard of living in your golden years.

Purpose And Scope Of This Chapter

This chapter focuses on the ongoing process of monitoring your retirement savings plan and making adjustments as needed to ensure it remains aligned with your evolving needs and life stages.

The Importance Of Regular Reviews And Re-Balancing

Just like a car needs regular maintenance, your retirement savings plan requires periodic reviews. Here's why regular reviews are crucial:

Assessing Progress: Track your progress towards your retirement goals. Are you on track to accumulate the desired amount by your target retirement date?

Evaluating Risk Tolerance: Your risk tolerance may change over time. As you approach retirement, you may prioritize income and stability over aggressive growth.

Re-balancing Your Portfolio: Market fluctuations can cause your asset allocation to drift from your target percentages. Regular re-balancing ensures your portfolio remains aligned with your risk tolerance and investment goals (Investopedia, 023).

Adapting To Changing Circumstances

Life throws curveballs, and your retirement plan may need adjustments due to unforeseen circumstances. Here are some examples:

Job Change or Salary Increase: A promotion or career change could impact your retirement savings potential. Adjust your contributions accordingly to maximize your retirement savings.

Unexpected Expenses: Major medical bills or unforeseen costs may require temporary adjustments to your savings contributions. Focus on getting back on track after the situation stabilizes.

Retirement Date Shift: You may decide to retire earlier or later than originally planned. Adjust your withdrawal strategy and savings goals accordingly.

Strategies For Monitoring And Adjusting Your Plan

Schedule Annual Reviews: Dedicate time at least once a year to review your retirement savings progress, risk tolerance, and asset allocation.

Utilize Online Tools: Many financial institutions and investment platforms offer online tools that allow you to track your progress and monitor your asset allocation.

Seek Professional Guidance: Consulting with a financial advisor at regular intervals can be beneficial, especially when navigating complex life changes or market fluctuations.

Building a secure retirement requires ongoing monitoring and adjustments. By scheduling regular reviews, re-balancing your portfolio as needed, and adapting to changing circumstances, you can ensure your retirement savings plan stays on track to deliver the financial security you deserve in your golden years. The following chapters will delve into the world of retirement income strategies and considerations, helping you translate your savings into a steady stream of income throughout your retirement.

CHAPTER 14

Reaping the Rewards
Securing Your Retirement Income

Congratulations! You've diligently saved and invested throughout your working years, building a solid foundation for your retirement. Now comes the crucial step: transforming your accumulated savings into a sustainable stream of income that allows you to enjoy your golden years without financial worry. This chapter explores strategies for creating a secure retirement income, managing inflation risk, and navigating market fluctuations to ensure your nest egg lasts throughout your retirement journey.

Why Retirement Savings Matter

Social Security alone is unlikely to maintain your desired lifestyle after retirement (Social Security Administration, 2023). A 2023 report by the National Institute on

Retirement Security (NIRS) highlights that nearly half of all pre-retirees (47%) are concerned about running out of money in retirement (National Institute on Retirement Security, 2023). Having a sustainable income stream from your retirement savings allows you to face retirement with confidence and financial independence.

Purpose And Scope Of This Chapter

This chapter focuses on the critical stage of converting your savings into a reliable income stream that supports your desired retirement lifestyle throughout your golden years.

Building A Sustainable Income Stream: Multiple Strategies For Your Consideration

There's no one-size-fits-all approach to generating retirement income. Here are some common strategies to consider, allowing you to customize a plan that aligns with your individual needs and risk tolerance:

Traditional IRA and Roth IRA Withdrawals: These retirement accounts allow for tax-advantaged withdrawals upon reaching retirement age. You can choose to withdraw a fixed monthly amount or take calculated withdrawals to maximize the longevity of your savings (The Motley Fool, 2023).

401(k) Withdrawals: Similar to IRAs, you can access your 401(k) funds upon reaching retirement age, typically with taxes applied to withdrawals. Some employers offer Roth 401(k) options, allowing for tax-free qualified withdrawals in retirement.

Social Security Benefits: Social Security provides a monthly benefit based on your lifetime earnings. You can choose to begin receiving benefits as early as age 62, but delaying benefits until full retirement age (FRA) typically results in a higher monthly payout (Social Security Administration, 2023).

Pensions: While less common, some employers offer traditional pension plans that provide a guaranteed monthly income stream in retirement.

Managing Inflation And Market Risks:

Inflation erodes the purchasing power of your money over time. Here are some strategies to combat inflation risk:

Invest in Assets with Inflation-Hedging Potential: Assets like certain stocks and TIPS (Treasury Inflation-Protected Securities) can offer some protection against inflation (Investopedia, 2023).

Consider a Fixed Annuity: Fixed annuities provide a guaranteed stream of income for a set period or lifetime, offering some stability against market fluctuations. However, be aware of surrender charges and other fees associated with annuities.

While market downturns are inevitable, a well-diversified portfolio can help weather these storms. Regular re-balancing and maintaining a long-term investment horizon are crucial for managing market risks.

Building a secure retirement income stream requires careful planning and diversification. By exploring various income-generating strategies, managing inflation risk, and employing sound investment principles, you can translate your retirement savings into a reliable income stream that allows you to enjoy a financially secure and fulfilling retirement. The following chapters will explore additional considerations and strategies to optimize your retirement journey, ensuring you can navigate unforeseen circumstances and maximize your enjoyment of your golden years.

CONCLUSION

"Secure Your Future: A Comprehensive Retirement Savings Guide" emphasizes the pivotal role of retirement savings in ensuring a secure and fulfilling retirement. The consequences of inadequate savings can range from financial vulnerability to compromised well-being, underscoring the necessity of prioritizing retirement planning.

Key Takeaways

Accurate Estimation of Expenses and Income: Understanding retirement expenses and sources of income is crucial for crafting a holistic retirement plan.

Employer-Sponsored Retirement Plans: Employer-sponsored plans are indispensable tools for retirement planning, offering benefits that individuals can leverage wisely.

Individual Retirement Accounts (IRAs): IRAs provide flexible and tax-efficient options for bolstering retirement savings, requiring a nuanced understanding of contribution limits and regulations.

Annuities and Alternative Income Sources: Annuities and alternative income sources provide stability and diversification in retirement income, necessitating informed decision-making.

Asset Allocation and Diversification: Balancing risk and return through asset allocation and diversification is fundamental for building a resilient retirement portfolio.

Risk Management: Implementing strategies like diversification and asset allocation helps mitigate risks and ensures a secure retirement.

Tax-Advantaged Retirement Accounts: Leveraging tax-advantaged accounts optimizes retirement savings by maximizing tax benefits.

Proactive Savings Strategies: Proactive approaches, such as catch-up contributions and maximizing employer benefits, accelerate retirement savings.

Fee Management: Minimizing fees and penalties maximizes the efficiency of retirement savings and investment growth.

Personalized Retirement Plans: Tailoring retirement savings plans to individual goals and circumstances ensures financial security and confidence.

Ongoing Monitoring and Adjustments: Regular reviews and adjustments to retirement plans maintain alignment with financial goals and changing circumstances.

Building a Secure Retirement Income Stream: Crafting a diverse and sustainable retirement income stream allows for a financially secure and fulfilling retirement.

Encouragement To Start Planning And Saving For Retirement

Embarking on the journey of retirement planning and saving is not only a prudent choice but also an essential step toward securing a gratifying future. By taking proactive measures to estimate expenses, explore retirement savings options, and implement personalized strategies, individuals can pave the way for a financially secure and fulfilling retirement. Regardless of age or financial situation, starting now and adapting along the way is key to building a robust retirement plan that aligns with personal goals and aspirations.

In conclusion, "Secure Your Future: A Comprehensive Retirement Savings Guide" serves as a roadmap for individuals seeking to navigate the complexities of retirement planning with confidence and foresight. By embracing the principles outlined in this guide and taking decisive action to secure their financial futures, readers can embark on a path toward a retirement characterized by stability, security, and fulfillment. Ultimately leading to a fulfilling and worry-free retirement.

GLOSSARY OF RETIREMENT SAVINGS TERMS

IRA (Individual Retirement Account): A tax-advantaged savings account designed to help individuals save for retirement.

401(k) Plan: An employer-sponsored retirement savings plan that allows employees to contribute a portion of their salary on a pre-tax basis.

Roth IRA: A type of individual retirement account that allows contributions to grow tax-free, with qualified withdrawals in retirement also tax-free.

Annuity: A financial product that provides a regular income stream in exchange for a lump sum payment or series of payments.

Asset Allocation: The process of distributing investments among different asset classes, such as stocks, bonds, and cash equivalents, to achieve desired risk and return objectives.

Diversification: spreading investments across different asset classes, industries, and geographic regions to reduce risk.

Inflation-Protected Securities (TIPS): bonds issued by the U.S. Treasury that are indexed to inflation to protect investors against purchasing power erosion.

Market Volatility: Fluctuations in stock prices and other financial instruments due to changes in economic conditions, investor sentiment, or geopolitical events.

Risk Tolerance: An investor's ability and willingness to endure fluctuations in the value of their investments.

Expense Ratio: The annual fee charged by mutual funds or exchange-traded funds (ETFs) to cover operating expenses.

Index Funds: Mutual funds or ETFs that passively track a particular market index, such as the S&P 500, with the goal of matching its performance.

Mutual funds are investment vehicles that pool money from multiple investors to purchase a diversified portfolio of securities.

REFERENCES

AARP. (2022). Retirement Expenses: What to Expect. Retrieved from

American Psychological Association. (2022). Stress in America: Coping with Change. Retrieved from

BLS (Bureau of Labor Statistics). (2022). Consumer Expenditure Survey.

Board of Governors of the Federal Reserve System. (2023). FOMC Statement on Economic Projections. Retrieved from https://www.federalreserve.gov/

Bawa, V. S. (2021). The role of diversification in portfolio risk management. *The Quarterly Review of Economics and Finance, 82*, 542-553.

Center for Retirement Research at Boston College. (2021). The State of Retirement in America. Retrieved from https://crr.bc.edu/

Employee Benefit Research Institute. (2022). EBRI Retirement Security Projections Model. Retrieved from https://www.ebri.org/

Employee Benefit Research Institute. (2022). Retirement Security Challenges Remain. Retrieved from https://www.ebri.org/

Federal Reserve. (2022). Report on the Economic Well-Being of U.S. Households.

Fernandes, V., &, Lusardi, A. (2023). Risk tolerance and retirement planning errors. *Journal of Pension Economics & Finance, 7*(3), 547-572.

Forbes. (2022). Annuities: A Guide to Understanding Your Options.

Forbes. (2022). How to Max Out Your 401(k) in 2022.

Forbes. (2022). Roth IRA Contribution Limits for 2022.

Gallup. (2022). Retirement Readiness.

ICI (Investment Company Institute). (2022). Retirement Accounts and Retirement Plan Assets. Retrieved from

Investopedia. (2023). Asset Allocation. Retrieved from https://www.investopedia.com/terms/a/assetallocation.asp

Investopedia. (2023). Rebalancing Your Portfolio. Retrieved from https://www.investopedia.com/terms/r/rebalancing.asp

Investopedia. (2023). Inflation-Protected Securities (TIPS). Retrieved from https://www.investopedia.com/terms/i/inflationprotectedsecurities.asp

Investopedia. (2023). Asset Allocation. Retrieved from https://www.investopedia.com/terms/a/assetallocation.asp

Investopedia. (2023). Exchange-Traded Funds (ETFs). Retrieved from https://www.investopedia.com/terms/e/etf.asp

Investopedia. (2023). Index Funds vs. Actively Managed Funds. Retrieved from https://www.investopedia.com/terms/i/indexfund.asp

IRS (Internal Revenue Service). (2022). Individual Retirement Arrangements (IRAs).

IRS (Internal Revenue Service). (2022). Retirement Plans.

IRS (Internal Revenue Service). (2023). 401(k) Plans. Retrieved from https://www.irs.gov/

IRS (Internal Revenue Service). (2023). Traditional IRAs. Retrieved from https://www.irs.gov/

IRS (Internal Revenue Service). (2023). Roth IRAs. Retrieved from https://www.irs.gov/

Kijakazi, K. (2022). The Importance of Retirement Savings. *Forbes*.

Kiplinger. (2022). Fixed Annuities: A Predictable Income Stream.

National Institute on Retirement Security. (2022). How Much Savings Do You Need to Retire?. Retrieved from https://www.nirsonline.org/

NerdWallet. (2022). Retirement Costs: How Much Do You Need?.

PBS (Public Broadcasting Service). (2022). Pensions: A Guaranteed Income Stream.

Pew Research Center. (2023). Retirement insecurity on the rise among older adults. Retrieved from https://www.pewresearch.org/

Retirement Income Institute. (2022). How Much Will Your Healthcare Cost in Retirement?.

Schwab, C. (2023). How to Manage Market Volatility. Retrieved from https://www.schwab.com/

Social Security Administration. (2023). Social Security Benefits. Retrieved from https://www.ssa.gov/

Society of Actuaries. (2023,). Living to 100: Demographics and Financial Implications for Retirement. Retrieved from https://www.soa.org/

The Motley Fool. (2023). Roth IRA Conversions: A Guide for 2023. Retrieved from https://www.fool.com/

The Motley Fool. (2023). Best Assets to Hedge Against Inflation. Retrieved from https://www.fool.com/

The Motley Fool. (2023). How to Withdraw Money from Your IRA.

The Motley Fool. (2023). Expense Ratio Definition.

Transamerica Center for Retirement Studies. (2022). 20th Annual Retirement Survey. Retrieved from https://www.transamerica.com/

AFTERWORD

Congratulations on completing "Secure Your Future: A Comprehensive Retirement Savings Guide." I hope you found the information within these pages helpful and empowering as you embark on your journey toward financial security in retirement.

Remember, the key to a successful retirement is proactive planning and continuous learning. While this guide provides valuable insights and strategies, it's just the beginning of your retirement planning journey. I encourage you to continue exploring and educating yourself about various retirement savings options, investment strategies, and financial planning principles.

Additionally, don't hesitate to seek guidance from financial advisors or retirement planning professionals. They can offer personalized advice tailored to your unique financial situation and goals.

As you move forward, keep in mind that retirement planning is not a one-time event—it's an ongoing process. Regularly review your financial goals, monitor your progress, and make adjustments as needed to stay on track.

Above all, remember that the decisions you make today will shape your future tomorrow. By taking proactive steps to secure your financial future now, you're setting yourself up for a retirement filled with peace of mind and fulfillment.

Thank you for choosing "Secure Your Future" as your guide. I wish you all the best on your journey toward a secure and fulfilling retirement.

Warm regards,

Suze Kaufman.

ABOUT THE AUTHOR
Suze Kaufman

Suze Kaufman is a passionate advocate for financial literacy and empowerment. With a love for the finance industry, Suze has dedicated her career to helping individuals achieve their financial goals and secure their futures.

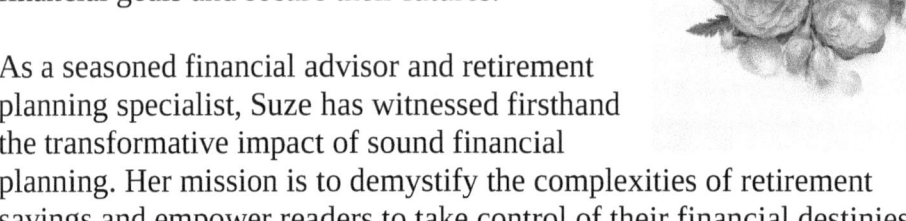

As a seasoned financial advisor and retirement planning specialist, Suze has witnessed firsthand the transformative impact of sound financial planning. Her mission is to demystify the complexities of retirement savings and empower readers to take control of their financial destinies.

Through her accessible writing style and comprehensive approach, Suze seeks to make retirement planning understandable and achievable for readers of all backgrounds and experience levels. "Secure Your Future: A Comprehensive Retirement Savings Guide" is the culmination of her expertise and dedication to helping others build a brighter financial future.

When she's not writing or advising clients, Suze enjoys spending time with her family, traveling, and exploring new culinary delights. She resides in the beautiful Pacific Northwest, where she finds inspiration in the natural beauty that surrounds her.

www.ingramcontent.com/pod-product-compliance
Lightning Source LLC
Chambersburg PA
CBHW050324230526
45471CB00005B/2333